ASPECTS
BETWEEN
SIGNS

SOPHIA MASON

ISBN-13: 978-0-86690-360-8

Cover Design: Jack Cipolla

Published by:
American Federation of Astrologers, Inc.
6535 S. Rural Road
Tempe, AZ 85283

www.astrologers.com

CONTENTS

INTRODUCTION

A great number of books have been written on the subject of aspects between planets, but very little has been written on understanding the external and psychological influence on aspects between signs containing the planets in aspect with one another.

The planetary energies are not taken into consideration in this book. The main concern is the motivational workings of aspects between signs in which the natal or progressed planets are positioned.

When considering orbs, use whatever orb that works best for you. Generally, this is six to eight degrees.

All major aspect between signs have been delineated and can be applied to the following:

1. Aspects between signs in the natal chart.

2. Aspects between signs from progressed planets to natal planets.

3. Aspects between signs in the solar return chart.

4. Aspects between signs in the diurnal chart.

5. Aspects between signs from lunation (New, Full, and Quarter Moon) positions to natal and progressed planetary positions.

6. Aspects between signs from solar and lunar eclipse positions to natal and progressed planetary positions.

7. Transiting major planets and their sign position in aspect with natal and progressed planetary positions.

INTRODUCTION

Chapter One

ARIES

Aries is cardinal and fiery, denoting ambition, energy, initiative, planning ability, and a pioneering spirit. The nature is impatient, impulsive, and impetuous. The urge is to instigate action rather than wait for matters to develop on their own. There is a strong desire to lead others or to hold a position of authority. The sign Aries represents the individual and his or her personal needs and desires.

An Aries Planet Conjunction a Planet, Midheaven or Ascendant in Aries

This configuration adds force, guts, energy, aggressiveness, initiative, and daring. With favorable aspects from other planets, this placement is excellent for promotion work, advertising, publications, creative ideas and a strong interest in new and undeveloped ideas, situations, or territories. There is a trigger-action mentality. The mind is quick to grasp new ideas and knows full well how to express them. Aries is attracted to anything that has a hint of challenge to it.

Unfavorable aspects to this conjunction can give the native a short temper. The nature is overly aggressive, highly impulsive, impetuous, and arrogant with the tendency to overreact without proper forethought.

In forecasting, the lunation or transiting planet in conjunction with a natal or progressed planet can be exciting or problematic. Much depends upon the type of aspects this conjunction makes to or receives from other planets.

In the positive sense, there is a spirit of new enterprise, accomplishments, excitement, and action. Plenty of energy will be required for some new undertaking. The native feels an urge to do something constructive and is ready for action.

Negatively, this aspect can produce wasted energy through impulsive actions. There is an urge to quarrel or to agitate others, danger of accidents or injuries to the head, and muscular aches and pains, fever, infections, and cuts or burns.

An Aries Planet Sextile a Planet, Midheaven, or Ascendant in Gemini

There is quickness of speech and mental activity. These individuals have the capacity to get ideas across to others. Good for salesmanship and in vocations where there is a quick turnover of affairs, these people have excellent powers of observation and judgment and are often witty conversationalists. This is an excellent combination for writing, teaching, lecturing, and administrative positions (Aries) in the educational field (Gemini).

There is easy rapport in communicating with others. However, should one of the planets positioned in Aries or Gemini be in a water house (fourth, eighth, or twelfth), this aspect is more likely to manifest itself inwardly and mentally, rather than verbally because these are the mute houses.

This aspect is good for manual dexterity and skills required in trades dealing with the auto industry, manufacturing or technical work.

In forecasting, the lunation or transiting planet in Aries sextile a natal or progressed planet denotes a period of much mental activity, and all forms of communication will require attention.

Short trips and pleasant visits with neighbors, close relatives, or friends are possible, and new ideas concerning future ventures can be developed at this time.

An Aries Planet Square a Planet, Midheaven or Ascendant in Cancer

This is somewhat of a difficult aspect to have in one's natal chart. The Cancer nature is water and the Aries nature is fire—two elements that do not mix—so the will is influenced by feeling. The subject leads an intense, emotional life colored by variable moods and impulsive behavior. From time to time there will be periods of emotional outbursts or hypersensitivity. This is further aggravated by explosive tempers and impatience.

The psychological influence is rather complex. On one hand, there is a tendency toward a frank and outspoken manner, often hurting others through a lack of tact and understanding. Yet, on the other hand, when these people are on the receiving end, they will withdraw at the first hint of criticism or reproach and recede into a protective, invisible shell.

These natives are extremely independent (both being cardinal signs) and should seek a career where they can be the boss. Either sex will require an understanding marriage partner who will recognize and accept their rebellion against restriction.

In forecasting, the lunation or transiting planet in Aries square a natal or progressed planet in Cancer can indicate problematic conditions with family members. Aries promises a new undertaking, experience, or event with much activity required. However, cooperation from family members may be lacking. It thus might be best to go it alone in order to avoid possible quarrels.

An Aries Planet Trine a Planet, Midheaven or Ascendant in Leo

This aspect offers much in the way of self-confidence and self-assurance because the ego is at its best here. There is also good athletic ability or an interest in other physical activities. These natives thrive on competition, but they're more interested in the pursuit of their own interests than those of others, so individual sports and activities would be more appealing than those involving a team.

Ambitious and industrious with the desire to lead and exercise power over others, there is a strong sense of justice, honor, fair play, and integrity. This aspect confers a decisive mentality and an intelligence that has the capacity to initiate projects on a constructive level. There is good mechanical, engineering, and teaching ability, as well as boundless energy, courage, determination, and vitality. In a male's chart this aspect endows masculinity and virility.

There is strong will in overcoming obstacles, difficulties in life, and health problems. For one to achieve recognition and advancement in life, personal efforts are generally required.

In forecasting, the lunation or transiting planet positioned in Aries in trine aspect with a natal or progressed planet in Leo denotes a period of progressive energy toward a desired goal.

This is a favorable period for entering into new projects. Work performance is at a high peak and dealt with efficiently, with long range plans in view. This is a time to contact important and prominent individuals who can help promote future growth. Obstacles and difficulties that have previously held you back can now be overcome with surprising ease.

If your child is participating in a school sporting activity, chances are his or her team stands an excellent chance of winning.

Aries Planet Quincunx a Planet, Midheaven or Ascendant in Virgo

The energy of the Aries sign in quincunx aspect with a planet in Virgo may give the tendency to be impatient, critical, and faultfinding with others. The pioneering spirit of Aries may abound with new and constructive ideas and powers of thought. However, these ideas may not be well received due to the frank and outspoken manner in which they were presented.

The individual with this aspect needs to cultivate patience and tact in dealing with others because the energy of Aries combined with the nervous sign Virgo often gives way to rash behavior coupled with a complaining or grumbling nature. The end result can reflect itself through stomach disorders, ulcers, or intestinal upsets.

In forecasting, the lunation or transiting planet in Aries in quincunx aspect with a natal or progressed planet in Virgo can bring contradicting issues in the way one handles work details.

There can be adverse criticism and/or faultfinding of work-related duties and irritating problems with coworkers or subordinates. It is best to try to avoid arguments and disagreements with those you work with.

A workplace accident is possible because of carelessness while handling machinery or tools, and dissentient circumstances can arise among workers, unions, contracts, and corporate matters.

An Aries Planet Opposition a Planet, Midheaven or Ascendant in Libra

This is a decision-making aspect. It can also bring about circumstances or events in which one person must contend with or yield to the wishes of another.

Libra wants to achieve a sense of balance in everyday existence through the maintenance of peace and harmony. Aries tends to create the opposite effect through lack of tolerance and patience.

The themes are compromise and a willingness to sacrifice one's principle from time to time. This native must learn to handle relationships with tact, diplomacy, and patience, and until this is achieved, there will be problems through the forming of partnerships in business and marriage.

In forecasting, the lunation in Aries in opposition with a natal, progressed, or transiting planet in Libra often produces conflicts with another party. If handled correctly, the opposition can result in a balance of opposing forces, resulting in cooperative and mutual agreements or activities. Therefore, this aspect can result in either a separation or a culmination of a fulfillment.

Encounters with another individual are often experienced with an opposition between Aries and Libra, and one may not see eye-to-eye with another person. Police activity can occur, resulting in litigation.

An Aries Planet Quincunx a Planet, Midheaven or Ascendant in Scorpio

A planet positioned in Scorpio likes to be in control of situations, job positions, and people. A planet in the independent, leadership sign of Aries can instill a rather aggressive, domineering, bossy, or dictatorial attitude toward these conditions.

The individual can invest effort in attaining his or her objectives through the use of brutal or ruthless behavior, and frankness coupled with sarcasm results in opposing forces and unpopularity. These individuals often feel that they have to do the job themselves in order to get it done right, thus creating more work and laborious efforts than necessary.

In forecasting, an opportunity may arise to gain financial rewards through the use of underhanded tactics.

There is a possibility of quarrels, injury, or accidents, and rebelliousness through the intervention of another party who may try to change your job status, seniority rights, or compensation.

This aspect can produce conditions or circumstances that call for much discrimination, and can indicate contacts or events that may affect the health or employment.

One may deplete the energy through overtime and hard work;

however, the financial benefit won't be worth the benefit if the end result is a physical breakdown.

An Aries Planet Trine a Planet, Midheaven or Ascendant in Sagittarius

This aspect endows a deep sense of pride in oneself, along with much self-confidence, idealism, physical strength, and a sense of honor. There is frankness and a tendency to be outspoken without the direct intention of hurting another. It generally indicates a good-humored, easygoing person with much enthusiasm, optimism, and leadership ability.

Luck plays an important role, often placing the native in the right place at the right time whenever the opportunity presents itself.

Men of wealth, influence, or religious and legal backgrounds may benefit the native from time to time.

In forecasting, this is an excellent time to sign contracts, handle legal affairs, and to reach agreements or settlements. There is a possibility for travel or contacts with those at a distance, marriage plans, becoming engaged, or hearing of a birth.

This indicates success in personal endeavors, fortunate business dealings, and the possibility of entering into new ventures, future expansion, or the realization of plans.

Assistance is possible through influential, wealthy, or educated individuals, as well as those affiliated with the government and legal or religious professions.

An Aries Planet Square a Planet, Midheaven or Ascendant in Capricorn

This aspect is not emotional like the Aries-Cancer square because Capricorn is reserved, controlled, and ambitious. These natives are not afraid of hard, dangerous, or dirty work as long as it promises to improve their career or lot in life. Personal ambitions may be thwarted by others or held in check through delays or circumstances beyond their control. This is an excellent configuration for the military or a political career.

This can be a dangerous, accident-prone aspect, one with harmful or destructive energies because the ruler of Aries is Mars and the ruler of Capricorn is Saturn, both of which are considered malefics.

There is a certain degree of restlessness that needs direction and control. These individuals tend to become overly enthusiastic about certain projects and then suddenly lose interest and drop the entire matter, blowing from hot to cold.

There is also a deep-rooted inferiority complex that may have stemmed from a parent's constant belittling or degrading attitude toward the individual. This can prevent the native from effectively expressing himself or herself emotionally with the opposite sex. In a male's chart, this can lead to sexual impotence, and in a female's chart it can indicate experiences with men who have sexual or emotional hang-ups.

There can be periodical outbursts of temper and a rebellious attitude toward those whom they feel are trying to dominate them, especially older people, parents, bosses, government employees, and men of authority over the native.

It would be wise for these individuals to seek a business of their own or to pursue a career that involves little contact with superiors. These natives cannot tolerate anyone constantly bossing them or closely monitoring their work.

In forecasting, impatience (Aries) through possible delay (Capricorn) may have you butting your head against a stone wall. You may retaliate in anger from frustration. Overreaction can lead to accidents, illnesses that are stress related, resentment toward those in authority and mental depression, or a personal sense of failure.

Aries governs new ventures and undertakings, while Capricorn represents old, stagnant conditions. Snags may develop when trying to break in to new and undeveloped territories. Or you may feel an urge to break away from old conditions.

It is best to put aside for the time being all major decisions and stick with routine duties. Poor judgment and hasty actions can result in business losses. Instead, direct the Aries energy to clearing out of clutter from the basement (Capricorn), attic, or garage.

An Aries Planet Sextile a Planet, Midheaven or Ascendant in Aquarius

This endows an excellent aptitude for fields such as mechanical, technical, scientific, aviation, and astrology, or a leadership position in a club or organization. The individual may be motivated to work with groups and associations. There is a fondness for friendships and the ability to get along well with them.

A love of freedom, decisiveness, strong willpower, and self-reliance are all characteristic of this aspect. There may be inventive ideas along new lines of endeavor. Once the mind is set toward a certain goal, it is very difficult to try to change a course of action. These natives are often excellent speakers.

In forecasting, you may experience sudden, new, exciting, and unexpected events. Success can be achieved through spontaneous energy, actions, or decisions involving friends and groups.

There can be personal involvement of an unexpected nature surrounding, clubs, organizations, or groups.

These natives may find themselves in an extraordinary situation calling for an exertion of energy directed toward a unique situation.

There can be surprising protection and luck involving an unexpected close call, possibly one that could have led to a serious accident.

Chapter Two

TAURUS

Taurus is earthy and fixed, denoting practicality, stability, caution, and reliability coupled with determination to put ideas across and stick with projects to the finish. These individuals have the perseverance to plan ahead and to work slowly toward a given goal. Somewhat methodical in their attitude and approach to life, they prefer to stick to daily routines. Security, money, and material possessions are of paramount importance because of the personal comforts derived from them.

A Taurus Planet Conjunction a Planet, Midheaven or Ascendant in Taurus

This configuration adds a greater degree of stubbornness, determination, and fixity of purpose. It is peace and harmony above all else, even if one must subject oneself to the will of another. Added emphasis is placed on money, material possessions, and secure circumstances.

Unfavorable aspects to this conjunction can create extravagance and overindulgence, as well as possible trouble through monetary affairs, obstinacy, and a love of pompous display.

In forecasting, the lunation or transiting planet in conjunction with a natal or progressed planet in Taurus can bring monetary gain or loss. Much depends upon the type of aspect this conjunction makes to or receives from other planets. Money will be of prime concern during this period.

This is a good time to become goal-oriented and to determine just what it is you want out of life. Review your expenditures and decide where you can combat extravagance. Explore new options for saving and investing and improvise new budget controls.

Negatively, you may go on a spending spree, making purchases that you later regret. There can be unyielding stubbornness toward a new situation that seems destined to undermine your routine and complacency.

A Taurus Planet Sextile a Planet, Midheaven or Ascendant in Cancer

Taurus and Cancer are very domesticated and practical signs that endow a subconscious desire to own property free and clear of mortgage payments. There is good judgment concerning material values and money along with the hope of achieving financial security. The nature is well-mannered, gentle, refined, affectionate, sociable, cheerful, and sympathetic. Often developed is a taste for good music and artistic endeavors.

This placement is excellent for careers in banking, real estate, farming, finance, and hospitality, including any financial career that allows these natives to work with the common people. The most important issue of this aspect is the strong need and desire for financial security and protective care of family members.

In forecasting, the lunation or transiting planet in Taurus sextile a natal or progressed planet in Cancer is good for business prosperity and monetary gains. There is a possibility for financial gain through food, home products, and real estate. One may receive a gift from another who has a Cancer or Taurus coloring.

Money could be refunded because of the overpayment of a bill connected with property, such as overpayment of a utility bill or a decrease in property taxes or insurance.

You could receive an invitation to an enjoyable social function, and this is an excellent period for home decorating and purchasing furniture, window treatments, and anything that will enhance the immediate environment.

A Taurus Planet Square a Planet, Midheaven or Ascendant in Leo

Both of these signs are of a fixed nature, endowing much in the way of obstinate pride. The nature may be resentful, extravagant, and overly fond of pleasure. Taurus has rulership over the emotions and Leo governs romance, so a square between these two signs can produce difficulty in love relationships. Be careful not to be too generous in these matters. Children can also be a source of financial expense and drain.

Natives with this aspect should guard against obesity and damaging the health through overindulgence.

In forecasting, a lunation or transiting planet in Taurus square a natal or progressed planet in Leo may indicate problematic conditions with a child and money.

Avoid extravagant purchases at this time, resist a stubborn attitude toward a changing condition, and loan nothing that you expect to be returned at a later time.

If this aspect occurs at the time of a solar or lunar eclipse or with heavy transits in effect, it is possible that someone in the immediate circle may suffer a heart attack.

A Taurus Planet Trine a Planet, Midheaven or Ascendant in Virgo

This is an excellent combination for discriminating handling of financial situations or affairs. Writing or teaching professions can prove satisfying. You have a natural talent for getting ideas across to others, and you are careful in what you say or write and take the time to adequately prepare yourself in order to avoid the possibility of criticism from others. Those you work with approve of the careful and methodical way you handle details. You can excel in any field requiring good judgment, such as accounting, clerical work, banking, real estate, nursing, or science.

Money may be spent on or earned through health foods, health products and hygiene paraphernalia. You can work well alone if necessary and without supervision. You will give those you work with the benefit of the doubt when there are differences of opinions. Viewing both sides of an issue is important because you want to be fair in reaching decisions.

In forecasting, the lunation or transiting planet in Taurus trine a natal or progressed planet in Virgo is an excellent time to purchase clothes that one will wear to work or want for practical purposes and good wearability.

Financial gain is possible through matters related to health, such as a refund check from a physician or insurance company or news that a dental or medical expense will be covered by your insurance. General indications are possible improvements in work-related details and duties or a financial increase through a raise or bonus.

Should one be self-employed, this aspect can bring about a serious attitude and thoroughness toward one's business. There may be a desire to contemplate new ideas for improving work efficiency, and a greater sense of awareness for details, neatness, and order. Office equipment or tools for work may be purchased.

A Taurus Planet Quincunx a Planet, Midheaven or Ascendant in Libra

A quincunx aspect indicates conditions and circumstances that often require personal service or self-sacrifice. It is indicative of events, contacts, or individuals who may directly or indirectly affect one's health or employment conditions.

Because both Taurus and Libra are ruled by Venus, one would

think that these signs would be compatible; however, earth (Taurus) and air (Libra) are not harmonious. This can bring problematic financial conditions through a marriage or business partner. There may be an easy come-easy go attitude with money and possessions, a tendency to be extravagant, and a love of fine clothing and rich living.

There is a strong desire for a peaceful, loving existence, harmony and happiness in marriage, and sociability with others. However, there seems to be a drawback that holds these individuals back from achieving these very things. They may marry people who do not earn enough to satisfy their expensive taste. In many cases there is an inability to communicate with the opposite sex.

In forecasting, the lunation or transiting planet in Taurus in quincunx aspect with a natal or progressed planet in Libra can indicate trouble with marriage or business partners regarding finances.

A financial compromise may be in order when others come into the picture, and additional services and self-sacrifices may be required. You may have to put in more time and effort without monetary rewards. Other people seem to expect more for their money for the same services rendered to them in the past.

Litigation can surround personal finances or material possessions. Perhaps you find that someone has been stealing from you and an injunction is filed against the person. In one way or another, it is possible that you might have to sign legal documents in connection with personal finances.

A Taurus Planet Opposition a Planet, Midheaven or Ascendant in Scorpio

Both signs have rulership over finances, and an opposition between these two money signs can indicate conflict and possible monetary loss. If one learns to compromise, there can be a blending balance of the two, resulting in cooperative handling of finances. There is a possibility for difficulty through inheritance, taxes, insurance, joint monetary situations, child support, and spousal maintenance.

Both signs tend to display a high degree of emotional intensity. If not kept under control, this can lead to a degrading sexual relationship, or one of the parties could indulge in a secret intrigue. Difficulties related to sexual matters can lead to separation or divorce, and very often these emotional experiences leave a feeling of general distrust of the opposite sex.

There is a tendency for one of the parties to display a dictatorial attitude toward the other, such as making excessive demands on the partner or the partner displaying a possessive attitude toward the native.

In forecasting, the lunation or transiting planet in Taurus in opposition with a natal or progressed planet in Scorpio can indicate a strong difference of opinions with another person, especially with someone of a Scorpio coloring (Scorpio Sun, Scorpio Ascendant, or Scorpio Moon).

Your earnings may be reduced to a lesser amount due to a cutback in hours or a temporary layoff. Money formerly expected through insurance companies, health benefits, social security, child support, or spousal maintenance could hit a snag or be delayed.

Scorpio can bring final endings, changes, separation of ties, and cutting off of relationships. For the time being, try to maintain a detached expression of feelings and keep the emotions under control. Otherwise, you may regret the drastic consequences of your actions.

A Taurus Planet Quincunx a Planet, Midheaven or Ascendant in Sagittarius

The individual may feel the pull between seeking personal and emotional satisfaction and operating on an impersonal, sociable, and intellectual level. Sagittarius represents a moralistic and religious tone that may have been instilled into the individual's background through early training. The pull toward trying to control the sensual and romantic desires of Taurus can cause deep-rooted emotional problems.

These natives tend to underestimate themselves, their capabilities, and self-worth. As a result, they could try to buy the affection and admiration of others through generous gifts, favors, or personal sacrifices. People can easily take unfair advantage of this proffered generosity.

In forecasting, personal sacrifice could be required, either through volunteering your valuable time or through assistance with money. Avoid insincere and extravagant promises to others that you are unable to fulfill. Your intentions might be honorable, but procrastination can interfere.

Inroads on your time or money through religious or charitable organizations are possible. You could hear troubling news from in-laws, friends, or relatives living in a distant city, who may be confronted with financial setbacks.

A Taurus Planet Trine a Planet, Midheaven or Ascendant in Capricorn

The Taurus sign is creative and the Capricorn sign represents practicality. A trine between these two signs endows one with an artistic flair that can be instilled into the career. Such may be the case with designers, architects, engineers, and carpenters.

This is an excellent combination for political careers or working for municipal government agencies. A parent, boss, or a figure of authority may be of some financial aid or benefit. These individuals have sound business sense with excellent organizational and planning ability. The nature is frugal, faithful, reserved, refined, modest, and morally correct.

In forecasting, the lunation or transiting planet in Taurus trine a natal or progressed planet in Capricorn can instill a desire for entering into some creative pursuits, especially those dealing with flower arranging, artworks, or furniture refinishing.

An increase in earnings is possible through recognition of past efforts or the assuming of additional responsibilities.

Money that someone owes you from the past or payments of overdue accounts will now be forthcoming. A gift is possible from an older person, a parent, or through a figure of authority.

A Taurus Planet Square a Planet, Midheaven or Ascendant in Aquarius

A square aspect between socially-orientated Taurus and idealistic, humanitarian Aquarius often creates a desire to write a book or invent something that will benefit mankind.

Should this square aspect between Taurus and Aquarius receive a sextile or trine from another planet, creativity in the way of humanitarian interests will be of a practical and workable idea.

However, there may be setbacks in the presentation of these projects. Other people may try to discourage the native by declaring the idea unfeasible. This can be most frustrating as fixed signs can become obsessive in their beliefs.

Because of the stubborn quality of both signs, the emotions can become rigid and dogmatic, refusing to be rational. On one hand they desire love and affection; on the other hand they are afraid to give fully of themselves. Fear of losing their freedom may be the root of this problem.

In forecasting, the lunation or transiting planet in Taurus in square aspect with a natal or progressed planet in Aquarius may bring upsetting and unexpected expenditures.

One should guard against impractical schemes and impulsive spending on friends or social functions.

Lending or borrowing money or material possessions can lead

to loss of friendship when payment or return of article is not forthcoming.

A Taurus Planet Sextile a Planet, Midheaven or Ascendant in Pisces

This combination endows a good singing voice, dancing ability, or musical and artistic talents. Excellent for such fields as flower arranging, interior decorating, and designing, these natives may have a creative, active imagination.

Reliable and inspirational hunches often guide these natives in the proper handling of personal income and possessions.

The nature is gentle, careful of social graces, and well mannered. There is a strong emotional attraction for the opposite sex, seeking the ideal in romantic relationships.

In forecasting, the lunation or transiting planet in Taurus in sextile aspect with a natal or progressed planet in Pisces can be receptive in purchasing items of artistic and unusual quality.

You may get an inspirational insight for monetary gain. Money may be forthcoming through charitable organizations or church functions, such as a bingo game or a parish raffle ticket.

Money could be gained through a hidden resource or a lovely art object or a cherished photograph could be received.

For other Taurus aspects, please see the preceding sign.

Chapter Three

GEMINI

Gemini is mutable and air, denoting a quick mind that readily and rapidly picks up knowledge. These people have the ability to express themselves with ease through speech and the written word. The disposition is somewhat high strung, nervous, and changeable with a short attention span. They have a witty sense of humor, with versatility and vivaciousness.

A Gemini Planet Conjunction a Planet, Midheaven or Ascendant in Gemini

There is much mental and nervous energy, as well as speaking ability. If the conjunction is well aspected, it could be the making of a writer, salesperson, or teacher or someone in the communication field, such as radio or TV announcer.

Should the conjunction receive unfavorable aspects, there can be mental or nervous tension that could, if not kept in check, lead to a nervous breakdown. One should guard against unnecessary worry and fretting over insignificant matters.

In forecasting, the lunation or transiting planet in Gemini conjunction a natal or progressed planet in Gemini denotes a period during which a lot of energy will be consumed, along with much running about and communicating.

This is a good time to handle neglected correspondence. Make those much needed phone calls and contact close relatives and siblings. Return to school and embark on a new learning program. Take a short trip or buy yourself a book.

On the negative side, you may overdo it physically. Be careful while driving. Avoid signing important papers. Be ready to give assistance to close kin, if necessary.

A Gemini Planet Sextile a Planet, Midheaven or Ascendant in Leo

This is an excellent placement for teachers or those who work with children as they have the ability to communicate well with youngsters at their own level of understanding. The nature is quick-witted, ingenious, ambitious, creative, and intelligent with power of thought and good common sense.

These individuals are great mimics or may have an interest in the theater. There is potential for writing plays, short stories, and children's books.

In forecasting, this is a good time to present ideas to those in a position of authority. It is a busy month for conversation, communication, and making new acquaintances.

Possible short trips could be undertaken for pleasure, entertainment, sports, or gambling. Travel could be related to children, romance, or social functions.

A Gemini Planet Square a Planet, Midheaven or Ascendant in Virgo

As both signs are ruled by Mercury, there is a degree of restlessness and overstimulation of the nervous system and mentality. These people are critical, changeable, and indecisive, and may exercise poor judgment or tend to twist words, saying one thing but really meaning something else. There is hypersensitivity and some feel that all ill-stated remarks are being directed at them.

They can be worriers regarding trifling matters and be overly concerned about their health.

Unless Mercury is well aspected, the memory can be poor and the mind slow and forgetful with details. Some are muddled thinkers or those who are often misunderstood.

Interference from close kin, brothers, sisters, or neighbors can affect the health or work performance.

In forecasting, the lunation or transiting planet in Gemini in square aspect with a natal, progressed, or transiting planet in Virgo can bring problems with communication or disagreements in the handling of work-related duties.

Conflicts are possible with coworkers and employers or overwork may negatively impact the nervous system, creating health disorders.

Misunderstandings and loss of or delays in receiving messages or documents can create problems in performance of duties.

Errors on delivery receipts or mechanical trouble with transportation vehicles can delay messages and the shipment of goods or services.

Be wary of unfavorable gossip, rumors or news being circulated by coworkers or in connection with work responsibilities and unions.

Do not permit the meddling attempts of close kin or neighbors to interfere with work attendance or create personal health problems.

Animosity is possible surrounding your domestic pet or a neighbor's could result in police activity.

A Gemini Planet Trine a Planet, Midheaven or Ascendant in Libra

This aspect endows one with a quick, intelligent, well-balanced, and refined mind. These individuals have the ability to persuade or sway others through charm, tact, and diplomacy. They are the thinkers and the planners. It is not their nature to seek an objective by force as they are peace-loving people who prefer using gentle persuasion.

These natives love to socialize and entertain, especially with individuals who are stimulating conversationalists and eager to exchange ideas or views.

In forecasting, the lunation or transiting planet in Gemini in trine aspect with a natal, progressed, or transiting planet in Libra brings social invitations, enjoyable communications, or wedding announcements.

There is a possibility for an enjoyable short trip with a pleasant companion.

Romantic opportunities while attending a lecture, evening adult classes or through associations of an intellectual nature are possible.

This aspect is favored for successful dealings with women in general, either through communication or short trips.

A lovely greeting card or gift could be received, and sometimes love letters are exchanged.

A Gemini Planet Quincunx a Planet, Midheaven or Ascendant in Scorpio

These individuals are quick, restless, changeable, cunning, crafty, and aggressive, as well as revolutionary in their ideas and attitudes. They tend to scatter their forces, both mental and physical, often having two projects going on at the same time. Some natives are at odds with themselves, wanting one thing and yet also wanting the exact opposite. At times they tend to overestimate themselves.

There is a need for self-expression and they do so in unusual ways or with the use of bold, new expressions. The speech is usually tinged with sarcasm or vulgar or obnoxious statements that others find irritating. When desiring something to their advantage, they can become very convincing speakers.

These individuals can size up a situation quickly, detect their opponents' weaknesses and know full well how to use this knowledge to their own advantage. They may be quite talkative, but it is usually on a superficial level that serves as a smoke screen for the real information they are trying to ferret out of their opponents. At the same time, however, they proffer no information of their own.

In forecasting, the lunation or transiting planet in Gemini quincunx a natal or progressed planet in Scorpio reveals a situation in which one may face a disturbing mental or emotional crisis.

These natives should guard against extreme nervous irritability and tension. They may hear upsetting news or receive communication that requires a change or revision of personal plans.

Problems are possible in comprehending a situation involving insurance, taxes, contracts, joint finances, inheritance, or spousal maintenance, or disagreements with close kin over insurance, wills, and inheritance.

This is not the best time for signing agreements in relation to joint money, wills, insurance, or property of others because of secrecy or underhanded tactics that may surround these matters.

A Gemini Planet in Opposition to a Planet, Midheaven or Ascendant in Sagittarius

There is a noticeable degree of nervous tension and irritability, and a tendency to scatter the forces by tackling too many jobs at one time.

This opposition aspect endows mental (Gemini) expansiveness (Sagittarius) to the point where the individual may have grandiose ideas or make promises that he or she is unable to keep.

These individuals may talk excessively but tend to procrastinate when it is time to put some of that talk into action.

There is muddled or confused thinking and yet the individual may display a know-it-all attitude or one of intellectual snobbery. However, if called upon to defend or prove their knowledge, they become flustered and generally blurt out the truth, especially so under cross examination. This aspect can produce a brilliant intellectual mind if the native is able to control the restlessness and over-expansiveness produced by these two mutable signs.

There can be problems with brothers, sisters, neighbors, or in-laws. A legal entanglement is possible with the native's brother or sister, depending upon the aspects to Jupiter and the condition of the third or ninth house and its ruler.

These people should be careful of verbal or written statements and the signing of contracts in order to avoid problems with lawsuits.

In forecasting, the lunation or transiting planet in Gemini in opposition with a natal, progressed, or transiting planet in Sagittarius can trigger mental confusion or interference with logical thinking.

Be sure you are able to fulfill obligations before signing legal contracts or making verbal agreements. Make it a point to read the fine print in order to avoid misunderstandings. Thoughts or discussions of a lawsuit may come to the fore.

One tends to have an over-optimistic attitude concerning projects or situations. As a result, you may try to tackle more than what is possible to deliver.

Short or long distance travels may not work out as well as planned. Messages can be misplaced or communication can hit a snag. Be sure to double check time and dates of all appointments.

Difficulties can arise through close kin, in-laws, neighbors, foreigners, or individuals living in distant places.

A Gemini Planet Quincunx a Planet, Midheaven or Ascendant in Capricorn

The positive thinking of Gemini can be thwarted by the negative attitude of Capricorn, resulting in mental depression, a serious outlook, or a slowness in absorbing facts and figures.

Natives born with this aspect may hesitate or stammer before speaking. This is due to the cautiousness of Capricorn, stalling for time to adequately express an opinion on a subject. They can be melancholy at times and dwell on past happenings. Although they have depth of thought, there is difficulty in self-expression.

These individuals are responsible and serious, and careful, patient, and painstaking in detailed work. However, they can worry or fuss too much over insignificant matters.

The individual could be considered to be a loner because of preoccupation or getting wrapped up in his or her own thoughts and ideas. A narrow-minded or overly conservative attitude is possible, and the individual can easily fall into a rut because of an attraction to the methodical, routine, and comfortable side of life.

In forecasting, the lunation or transiting planet in Gemini quincunx a natal, progressed, or transiting planet in Capricorn can bring difficulty in the communication field.

News, communication, or documents (Gemini) that may be important to the job or career (Capricorn) cam be delayed, misplaced, or hampered in some way, causing difficulties with those in authority.

There may be quarrels, dissension, or separation through brothers, sisters, neighbors, or those who represent a figure of authority.

Bosses or parents may not be supportive when seeking favors or advancement. If running for a political office or reelection, there may be a lack of response from voters due to hindered communication.

Mental depression and dissatisfaction with one's job may require self-discipline in order to avoid doing something rash.

Parents can be a source of mental anguish or responsibility. A quincunx is an aspect of self-sacrifice and service to others. One may feel heavily burdened with services required, either to a parent or through bosses.

Important news, communication, or shipments may be delayed. Short trips can hit a snag as a result of detours or a vehicle breakdown.

A Gemini Planet Trine a Planet, Midheaven or Ascendant in Aquarius

This is an excellent configuration for the fields of communication, writing, teaching, lecturing, computer programing, electronics, the scientific, or astrology and the occult.

These individuals make excellent diplomats, public relation representatives, and customer service representatives, as well as any job or career that requires quickness of thought coupled with a gracious manner of speaking or greeting others.

Aquarius rules radio and television, so a trine from a planet in Gemini, governing communication, can give aspirations to be a radio or television announcer.

There can be emotional detachment (air signs), and many of these individuals are of high intellectual caliber. This, however, can interfere with domestic life, as these natives are far more concerned with the welfare of others than with family ties.

They possess originality and inventiveness with advanced ideas and thought, good intuition, and astuteness. There is a revolutionary spirit and the desire to be independent and they have the power to persuade and influence others.

In forecasting, a lunation in Gemini trine a natal, progressed, or transiting planet in Aquarius means unexpected and exciting news.

One may discover new or unique ways of improving work efficiency. News is possible related to a job involving electronics, imaging equipment, or radio or television.

Unexpected good news could be received, or unexpected short trips undertaken that prove to be exciting and interesting.

Good news concerning the affairs of brothers, sisters, or neighbors is possible, and this is a good time to attend astrology lectures or group activities of an intellectual nature.

A Gemini Planet Square a Planet, Midheaven or Ascendant in Pisces

Both signs are mutable and have learned to adapt when situations become unbearable. There is a certain degree of restlessness and nervousness of the mentality and physical condition.

Pisces often indicates psychological fears when afflicted. This may operate through the Gemini sign in which the native experiences difficulties in self-expression. In some cases these natives use alcoholic beverages as a crutch to help them overcome a sense of shyness or inhibition when speaking before large groups of people.

There is a tendency to escape from reality by building an unrealistic dream world. Although there is nothing wrong with periodic, mental escapism, problems begin when one starts to believe these self-created illusions.

These natives can be overly sensitive and lack self-confidence. As a result, they can distort the truth about themselves and mold a self-image that crumbles when confronted by facts.

In forecasting, a lunation or transiting planet in Gemini square a natal, progressed, or transiting planet in Pisces can introduce expansive and unrealistic theories.

Muddled or confused messages can be problematic in business or personal affairs.

Be careful what you say as you could reveal secret information to the wrong person. Use caution regarding important papers. Delay signing anything until after this aspect has passed. Disregard gossip and news from unreliable sources. Someone could purposely misrepresent the facts for fraudulent reasons.

You can be exploited, misguided, outsmarted, or hurt by opening yourself to the influence of other people. Maintaining your sense of logic is most important at this time.

Be mentally alert in handling and filling drug prescriptions. Make sure the pharmacist has not made an error in judgment.

If short trips are necessary, avoid daydreaming while driving. Unusual accidents can occur if you are not alert to surround conditions.

Siblings and neighbors could be a source of concern with their emotional problems or ill health.

For other Gemini aspects, please see the preceding signs.

Chapter Four

CANCER

Cancer is cardinal and watery, denoting the extreme sensitivity of these people to their environment and emotional feelings projected by others. Strongly domesticated with maternal and protective instincts, Cancer has a fear of rejection and ridicule that holds the native back from asserting himself or herself in achieving success in life. These people tend to brood over past happenings and imaginary slights as though each remark were directed personally at them. Sympathetic, friendly, and patient, they have an over-active imagination that needs control.

A Cancer Planet Conjunction a Planet, Midheaven or Ascendant in Cancer

There is a strong emphasis on the emotions, home, and desire for security. If the conjunction receives favorable aspects, there is caution, economy, sympathy, and an excellent memory. Unfavorable aspects to the conjunction from other planets can produce emotional upheaval, domestic strife, and lack of harmony with a parent.

In forecasting, the lunation or transiting planet in Cancer conjunction a natal or progressed planet can emphasize an emotional involvement with another individual. Circumstances or situations can be emotionally upsetting. Much depends upon the type of aspect this conjunction makes to or receives from other planets. The general trend is expressed through the home environment, the emotions, and family members. In the positive sense, this aspect can stimulate an interest in redecorating, enlarging the home, or the purchase and sale of property. Enjoyable family outings and cementing of family ties is possible.

A negative aspect can be very trying, emotional, and depressing. The home base undergoes troubling situations. Parents or older individuals pose a problem or are a source of concern and responsibility. Property or real estate taxes could be increased or repairs could be more costly than first anticipated.

A Cancer Planet Sextile a Planet, Midheaven or Ascendant in Virgo

Here we have two introverted, quiet signs, both loving seclusion. The emotional nature combines practicality and security to the best advantage. Never underestimate these individuals; they are quite shrewd in material matters.

They have excellent memory recall and the ability to communicate well with the general public. This can be a big advantage in careers dealing with real estate, public relations, teaching, food management, home furnishings, and related health fields.

The nature is thoughtful, tactful, and sympathetic with good judgment and discretion. Their manner of speaking is simple, plain, and direct. The emotions are usually well controlled.

In forecasting, the lunation or transiting planet in Cancer in sextile aspect with a natal, progressed, or transiting planet in Virgo is good for business ventures.

This is an excellent time to purchase book cases, office equipment, clothing, or articles to be used for working purposes.

Your good business sense at this time can bring favorable results through small transactions.

There is much activity in the form of written communication, short trips, business communication, and details to be handled in connection with unions, work, or health conditions. Enjoyable visits are possible with aunts, uncles, or coworkers. Someone older or mature will be of beneficial assistance in helping you find a job or making your present working area more efficient.

A Cancer Planet Square a Planet, Midheaven or Ascendant in Libra

The mentality of Libra is inhibited by the emotionalism of Cancer, creating unusual fears or phobias. The usual well-balanced mind of Libra can become hypersensitive or develop an inferiority complex. There can be a tendency to withdraw from normal relationships because of a fear of rejection. This psychological issue might stem from a childhood experience; possibly a parent or an older family member instilled this feeling of shyness or inadequacy. In any case, these natives seem to feel they cannot do as they please because of certain restrictions through others.

The nature is vulnerable and too trusting of others. As a result, these natives can suffer conflicts in love matters or experience difficulty in sexual relationships. There can be disharmonious relationships with the mother-in-law or other female relations through marriage.

In forecasting, there is the possibility of a tragic consequence or an emotional upset through a personal relationship.

Family gatherings or social activities can suffer an unfortunate change of events or circumstances. Emotional feelings are susceptible to family misunderstandings, and litigation is possible surrounding property or family members.

A Cancer Planet Trine a Planet, Midheaven or Ascendant in Scorpio

There is possessiveness and protectiveness of personal feelings and family matters. These individuals are shy, secretive, intensely emotional, and reserved, and prefer solitude. The psychic nature is strong with an intense interest in research of the occult or the unknown.

These individuals have a fanatical attitude in the pursuit of achievement in a particular field of endeavor. They can exercise a powerful influence on large groups through the spoken or written word.

In forecasting, the lunation or transiting planet in Cancer in trine aspect with a natal or progressed planet in Scorpio means a fanatical pursuit of a personal aim or objective.

This is an excellent time to change a personal bad habit or begin a diet. Gain is possible through the financial resources of others.

There is the possibility of fate (governed by Scorpio and Pluto) characterizing a major event—one that will alter circumstances or introduce a new relationship affecting the native in a personal and distinctive manner.

A Cancer Planet Quincunx a Planet, Midheaven or Ascendant in Sagittarius

This aspect is not overly harsh or difficult because the rulers, Moon and Jupiter, are not considered malefics. The sign Cancer enjoys dealing with the common people and in quincunx aspect with a planet in Sagittarius, there may be an interest in working with the underprivileged. A quincunx aspect requires one to be of service to others. However, know when to draw the line to prevent others from taking unfair advantage of you.

There may be emotional upsets or related problems with in-laws. Legal affairs can arise with family members over property, inheritance, or insurance. The emotional side of Cancer can distort the good judgment of the Sagittarius mentality, resulting in misplaced confidence or trust in others.

The nature is generally, sensitive, optimistic and kind. Upon occasion, however, the disposition can become changeable, irritable, restless, and argumentative.

In forecasting, the lunation or transiting planet in Cancer in quincunx aspect with a natal or progressed planet in Sagittarius brings possible concern of a family member living in a distant city or through relatives of the spouse.

Emotional problems of others or concerning one's family may work on your sympathy. You can overextend yourself by promising to help them. Legal difficulties can arise through family members or with property and real estate. Guard against an emotional crisis with someone of a foreign background.

Be careful with far-reaching plans in connection with purchasing or selling of a home or property. Moderation should be the key word if one is expanding the present residence or redecorating.

A Cancer Planet Opposition a Planet, Midheaven or Ascendant in Capricorn

This is one of the most ambitious combinations, but it can indicate conflict between affairs of the home and the career, as the individual can easily become a workaholic. The native can unconsciously replace a lack of emotional fulfillment with hard work.

This aspect has all the indications of one who is suffering from an inferiority complex. Environmental background or parental upbringing is often responsible for this feeling of emotional inhibition. A parent may have been rather rigid in attitude or a stern disciplinarian, unable to display affection. In some instances there may have been a loss or separation through a parent because of death or divorce. Much depends upon the condition of the natal Moon, Saturn, and the fourth or tenth house.

These natives are inclined to take life seriously. Hiding their true feelings and often apprehensive of close relationships, these natives can be rigid and lack flexibility. They must learn to bend and yield when the occasion calls for it. These natives can be moralistic to the extreme, and formal, reserved, and stiff to the point where others become uncomfortable in their presence. Emotional depression and a feeling of discontent is common.

In forecasting, the lunation or transiting planet in Cancer in opposition with a natal or progressed planet in Capricorn can bring added responsibility through a parent or through those in authority.

Family worries and separation of or trouble with the wife or mother are possible. This can be an emotionally depressing time coupled with lack of energy and a general rundown feeling. One feels unloved or neglected.

This is not the time to make decisions concerning emotional relationships, the wife, or mother. One may harbor thoughts of breaking away from these close ties.

Delays and hindrances are possible in the purchase, sale, or re-decoration of the home. Setbacks are possible in vocations dealing with real estate and food.

A Cancer Planet Quincunx a Planet, Midheaven or Ascendant in Aquarius

The emotional nature of Cancer is upset and perverted by the eccentric and strong-willed nature of the Aquarius coloring. These individuals can run the gamut of emotions from one extreme to the other. On one hand, the native desires dependency upon another, the domestic life, emotional fulfillment, and lasting attachments. Then, suddenly, the native jumps to the opposite side of the fence, demanding freedom, independence, and the need to be with friends.

This constant extreme of emotionalism can cause health disturbances through the nervous system. This is also an accident-prone aspect that can result in illnesses that are difficult to cure.

The nature is inventive, imaginative, intuitive, and creative. On impulse, they can extrude peculiar or eccentric behavior. Some may have an odd sense of humor.

In forecasting, the lunation or transiting planet in Cancer in quincunx aspect with a natal, progressed, or transiting planet in Aquarius indicates sudden and unusual events requiring a disturbing change of plans.

Guard against unexpected, emotional, and eccentric behavior. To do otherwise could result in unpredictable situations that could later prove embarrassing.

An emotional bond with a close friend could be severed through loss, separation, or misunderstandings.

A buildup of emotional tension is possible through interference of others or through circumstances. This is a highly excitable and restless period.

A Cancer Planet Trine a Planet, Midheaven or Ascendant in Pisces

Both signs are sensitive, emotional, sympathetic, quiet, and protective. There may be a strong interest in the occult or metaphysics and astrology, or an affinity for working with the sick, aged, or the mentally disturbed as in psychology and related subjects.

They have an uncanny way of placing themselves into other people's shoes and almost experiencing the emotions or problems of others.

The nature is gentle, kind, and sensitive. These people have excellent intuition or feelings of what is right and wrong, as well as the ability to visualize and mentally project a picture of what they want to do before putting it into action.

In forecasting, the lunation or transiting planet in Cancer in trine aspect with a natal or progressed planet in Pisces brings the possibility of psychic experiences or creative and inspirational ideas.

There can be unforeseen or hidden gains that will benefit family members. Past issues surrounding the home base or property can bring unusual and exciting developments.

Far-reaching wishes can now be achieved. Artistic talents or interests can be enhanced through enrollment in classes, or through the purchase of a musical instrument.

For other Cancer aspects, please see the preceding signs.

Chapter Five

LEO

L eo is fixed and fiery, denoting ambition, courage, initiative, action, and determination. There is a desire to hold a position of authority or a managerial post, as these people have strong leadership ability and strive for possessions and material gain. The nature is kind, generous, and sympathetic with the tendency to see only the good in others. Advancement in life is achieved through personal ability and application of energy.

A Leo Planet Conjunction a Planet, Midheaven or Ascendant in Leo

There is emphasis placed upon the ego, along with a marked degree of self-confidence, self-assuredness, and a desire for honor, fame, and recognition. Favorable aspects to this conjunction mean that the native has the ability to achieve a set goal in life.

Should the conjunction receive unfavorable aspects from other planets, the native should guard against vanity, boastfulness, and arrogance. The more this individual brags or appears conceited, the deeper is his or her inferiority complex and lack of confidence.

In forecasting, the lunation or transiting planet in Leo conjunction a natal or progressed planet denotes that children, love affairs, new undertakings, schools, and speculation will be of prime interest. In the positive sense, this is a great time to press ahead with plans for entertainment and affairs involving children, school programs, games, and romance. It is good for organizational ability and for seeking positions of trust and responsibility. Promotion to a management position or control of a department is possible.

In the negative sense, this aspect can mean problematic conditions concerning the affairs of children and schools, romance, and speculation. If other, heavy transits are in force at the same time, there is the possibility of losing a friend or family member through a heart condition or sudden events.

A Leo Planet Sextile a Planet, Midheaven or Ascendant in Libra

Both signs, Leo and Libra, are romantic to the extreme. The nature is endowed with warm-hearted affection, a strong ego, pride, and refinement of character, and there is a love for luxury, possessions, and beautiful objects. There is a noticeable youthfulness and attractiveness in appearance and personality. These natives can be diplomatic when the situation calls for it, tactful, warm, and friendly.

In forecasting, the lunation or transiting planet in Leo in sextile aspect with a natal or progressed planet in Libra is an excellent time for hosting parties and announcing engagements. Social activities can take an upward trend. Romance becomes an issue, either personally or indirectly. Children may announce their wedding plans.

You may have to assist a child in making the right contacts and associations that can help solve his or her problems. Situations surrounding children and litigation work out better than you had anticipated.

Artistic pursuits, music, or dancing take on new interests. Gifts may be received or exchanged.

A Leo Planet Square a Planet, Midheaven
or Ascendant in Scorpio

Both signs are fixed in their nature, endowing strong will and determination. Deep hurts with vindictive feelings over past romances are often experienced. There may be unwise action or overindulgence in sexual activities. Difficulties are possible in the rearing of children because of emotional or psychological problems on their part.

If the ruler of the fifth house or planets therein are malefics and make unfavorable aspects to the ruler of the eighth or planets therein, there could be a loss of a child through miscarriage. In some cases the native or the wife may be unable to bear children or have no desire for them.

The nature is to overdo and run unnecessary risks. These people are independent to the extreme and will not tolerate being bossed. It is difficult to understand these natives as they are secretive in personal affairs. They can be forceful and domineering, and may have a desire to rule or control others.

Affairs of children could be a source of financial loss and expense. It would be unwise to co-sign for children if they are seeking bank loans. You could lose an insurance policy because of careless actions of a child, and an upsetting experience with a place of entertainment could result in obtaining a settlement from the company's insurance company.

In forecasting, the lunation or transiting planet in Leo square a natal or progressed planet in Scorpio can brings adjustments and major changes as a result of upheavals concerning the affairs of children or a love relationship.

Fate is governed by Scorpio and Pluto. This aspect can produce a turning point in one's life. A child may be removed from one's life due to their moving away or leaving for college. A love relationship could be severed.

A child who is having difficulties with money they owe others could come to you for financial assistance. There could be a power struggle between you and a child. If unmarried, trouble, possessiveness, or an act of jealousy is possible through a love relationship.

Any legal action connected with the affairs of children in general has a beneficial way of working out.

Also, if you have legal action pending for a past eye or back injury, chances are the hearing or court action will be in your favor. Travel could be undertaken with a romantic interest, for entertainment reasons, or with a school program. Sporting events involving children and schools are favored.

A Leo Planet Trine a Planet, Midheaven or Ascendant in Sagittarius

The nature is charitable, sincere, frank, honorable, honest, and moral. These natives have the ability to influence others through the use of logic and abstract thought. This is an aspect of luck, as it providentially protects the native from want of anything. Whenever a particularly rough time faces this native, something occurs at the last minute that saves him or her.

Higher education, religion, travel, and legal action can have beneficial results for the native. There is the ability to get along well with people of all backgrounds, races, and religions. There is the possibility of gain or assistance from in-laws.

In forecasting, opportunities open up for future expansion, socially and financially. This is a lucky period for gambling and sports pools. A child who is in a distant city or away at college may visit you, or you could travel to visit him or her.

A Leo Planet Quincunx a Planet, Midheaven or Ascendant in Capricorn

This configuration can produce a hard worker with a firm conviction that responsibility to one's job should supersede all other matters. Often this is carried to the point where the native feels that no one else has the capacity to handle the details or work as efficiently as he or she. Bosses and superiors note these qualifications and take advantage of the native by placing additional burdens upon him or her. As a result, the native will begin to feel unappreciated and overworked.

There may be loss of or separation through a parent. Or one may have been too firm and restrictive in early training with little show of affection. A small family is associated with this aspect. The native may regard children as a serious burden and worry unnecessarily about them.

The nature is serious, moral, conservative, and conscientious. The native could be firm, unchangeable and unbending.

In forecasting, superiors, those in authority, or a parent could place additional burdens upon the native's shoulders. Long hours at work can have a negative affect upon the health. Be careful that you do not get so engrossed in what you are doing that you lose all concept of time. If chest pains develop, it may not be a heart condition but a warning that you are overdoing it.

The affairs of children, a love relationship, investments, and places of entertainment can have a depressing effect on the native. If heavy planets afflict at the same time, it is possible that an older member of the family suffers a heart attack or a stroke.

A Leo Planet Opposition a Planet, Midheaven or Ascendant in Aquarius

Because both signs are of a fixed quality there is determination to use mental (Aquarius) activity toward the betterment of mankind, often through scientific research or astrology. This aspect can endow a magnetic quality to the native's personality. These natives require an occupation that gives them freedom of action and thought.

If other aspects agree, there could be difficulties or a sudden separation through a love relationship, estrangements from children who may suddenly decide to leave home or move to another state, and unexpected loss of friends.

The nature is hypersensitive, overly independent, strong-willed, unpredictable, restless, and subjected to nervous trouble. Life seems to bring the element of unexpected events, causing one to break away from old ties and formulate new ones.

In forecasting, an opposition can bring separation through loved ones, children, and friends. Unexpected developments concerning investments or matters of entertainment and night-clubs are possible.

If one uses this opposition constructively, he or she can achieve a balance between the two, reaching a mutual agreement toward one common bond. Otherwise, the individual can create unexpected turmoil in a situation that he or she feels is restrictive.

A Leo Planet Quincunx a Planet, Midheaven or Ascendant in Pisces

There is the tendency to overdramatize romantic interludes or enjoy the intrigue of hidden affairs. Beware of deception, deceit, and chaotic conditions through others, especially with situations surrounding the affairs of children, romance, and investments.

Natives with this aspect should avoid overindulgence in alcohol or the abuse of habit-forming drugs that can have an adverse effect upon the health and personality. This is also an aspect of illnesses that are hard to detect or diagnose. The overly imaginative mind of Pisces can create a psychosomatic disorder involving the heart or eyes. Hypersensitivity to certain drugs or anesthetics could cause a temporary heart stoppage.

You may have a child who will have problems with his or her feet or be hypersensitive or allergic to certain foods or medication. The health of children should be guarded in their early years to protect them against possible diseases that can affect the heart. An enlarged heart is also possible.

In forecasting, be aware that there may be hidden factors surrounding the affairs of children. Be alert to possible drug abuse of children. One may enter the hospital for an illness that is hard to define. This is the time to be on your toes in regards children, even if they have never given you trouble in the past.

Sexual enthrallment or a secretive love relationship might appear to be exciting during this period. However, the emotional turmoil might not be worth it when the time comes to face reality.

For other Leo aspects, please see the preceding signs.

Chapter Six

VIRGO

Virgo is mutable and earthy, denoting practicality and discrimination. These people have the patience to apply methodical methods and painstaking details to their best advantage. There is a desire for knowledge and specialized skills.

The nature is diligent and correct with a sense of criticism and an analytical mind. Good opportunities are often missed due to the care and attention that is demanded of them from ill family members. Faultfinding is their main drawback.

A Virgo Planet Conjunction a Planet, Midheaven or Ascendant in Virgo

This conjunction emphasizes the discriminating facility of Virgo. If the conjunction receives favorable aspects, this can be productive for creativity on a practical level, such as dress-making, tailoring, cake decorating, and flower arranging. These people can excel in any field where painstaking details are a must, as in pharmacy, nursing, accounting, banking, and health care.

Should this conjunction receive unfavorable aspects from other planets, it can confer a faultfinding and critical attitude, changeability, and nervousness. Stomach tension, indigestion, and problems with ulcers when the immediate environment is upset and disturbed are possible.

In forecasting, the lunation or transiting planet in Virgo conjunction a natal or progressed planet means that working conditions, coworkers, aunts and uncles, and health conditions, your own or of others, will have to be dealt with.

In the positive sense, with good aspects, teamwork and cooperation from coworkers is favored. Seek the aid of officials if a job change is desired, and use methodical procedures to improve working conditions and tasks.

Negatively, with unfavorable aspects, you may have to perform a service for another individual or care for an ill family member. Job situations will undergo an unfavorable change. Dissention is possible with a coworker or supervisor is possible.

A Virgo Planet Sextile a Planet, Midheaven or Ascendant in Scorpio

This is an excellent position for those interested in occupations dealing with the medical field, such as physician, dietician, pharmacist, and nurse. Both signs are perfectionists and this may incline the native to be critical and faultfinding. These natives must realize that others do not possess this degree of perfection, so they should exercise tolerance and patience of friends and family members.

Both signs are introverted and negative, endowing a rather reserved, aloof and austere nature. It may be difficult to approach these natives or to understand them. They have the urge to dig deeply into projects that require careful study, preparation, and research. Most have an inquisitive mind and perseverance in solving difficult problems or arduous tasks.

In forecasting, the lunation or transiting planet in Virgo in sextile aspect with a natal or progressed planet in Scorpio can give a desire to pursue an objective with fanatical zeal.

This is a good time to make corrective and required changes in the work environment. You will have the ability to exercise an influence upon persons at work with favorable results. You should be able to cope with any situation requiring health care or services rendered to others. The attainment of success or advancement in work-related areas is possible, and there can be monetary gains through work.

A Virgo Planet Square a Planet, Midheaven or Ascendant in Sagittarius

There can be some form of conflict in the character traits, although not of a dangerous quality. Both signs are peaceful and adaptable. The Sagittarius element is abstract in thought, freedom-loving, and easygoing. The Virgo wants to break down into finer details the Sagittarius frank and fiery expressions. The end result is a critical and faultfinding nature. One that is careless of details and lacks organizational ability. These natives can be sloppy in personal appearance or hygiene. The nature is alert and impressionable, but there is liability toward deception and errors in judgment. Misinterpretation can be avoided by taking the time to check facts and figures before barging ahead.

There may be dissatisfaction or discontentment with or through in-laws. Lawsuits are possible through a pet or employees or because of working conditions.

In forecasting, the lunation or transiting planet in Virgo square a natal or progressed planet in Sagittarius means promises will be made that you cannot possibly keep. Take nothing for granted and guard your actions at work and with those whose background is different from your own.

Misrepresentation could surround legal activities and be blown out of proportion. You may have to file legal action against an employee or the company for discrimination or health conditions that occurred as a result of working conditions. Watch your pet and those of others to avoid legal entanglements. If you are dissatisfied with your job, be sure a superior will back you up before making waves.

A Virgo Planet Trine a Planet, Midheaven
or Ascendant in Capricorn

Both signs have an earthy, practical, and a scientific bent to their nature. There may be an interest in the healing professions or politics. Matters to do with advancement of one's career proceed with carefully designed long-range plans. Details are seldom overlooked and these people have the patience and the perseverance to wait for the final outcome of any venture.

These natives are reserved, aloof, and detached. They may have difficulty in expressing their emotions. There is good organizational ability. The nature is cautious, tactful, determined, and sensible, and moral character and self-control are good. They have an interest in cultural arts and associating with people of prestige.

In forecasting, the lunation or transiting planet in Virgo in trine aspect with a natal or progressed planet in Capricorn brings a possible advancement in one's career that has been long overdue.

This is one of the best aspects for communicating with superiors and presenting them with the facts and figures of past accomplishments, which can be to your advantage. If other major planets assist, this can be an aspect of retirement from one's career. Some find jobs with old, established companies, or with political parties. All matters that have been pending for some time concerning health or work will now culminate in a fruitful conclusion.

A Virgo Planet Quincunx a Planet, Midheaven
or Ascendant in Aquarius

Aquarius is a freedom-loving sign that does not like to conform to certain standards or be bogged down with boring routines. A quincunx aspect with Virgo, which represents an appreciation for the finer details and discipline, creates upsetting quirks in the personality. There is an inability to adjust to routine and regulated working habits.

There may be unsettling conditions with coworkers or employees (Virgo) because the native's attitude is unreliable and revolutionary (Aquarius). When work routines become boring, these natives like to instill crazy antics that upset and annoy coworkers.

In forecasting, the lunation or transiting planet in Virgo in quincunx aspect with a natal or progressed planet in Aquarius means that upsetting changes in work routines are possible, such as a change of shift or department. Whatever the cause, it will be a disliked change of routine.

For the time being, avoid coworkers who have a reputation for being eccentric. A friend (Aquarius) may become unexpectedly ill (Virgo).

A Virgo Planet Opposition a Planet, Midheaven or Ascendant in Pisces

Both signs are negative and introverted and work best by themselves and in solitude. A planet in Pisces can run the gamut of emotional extremes and despondency, resulting in self-pity or exaggerated concerns of health matters when opposed by a planet in Virgo. The nature lacks self-confidence, is easily discouraged, and should guard the thinking against impractical lines of thought and ideas.

It is best not to reveal personal and secretive affairs to coworkers. Hypersensitivity or allergy towards a certain food or medication is possible, and there can be a tendency for psychosomatic disorders, as well as sorrows through aunts, uncles, and small pets.

In forecasting, the lunation or transiting planet in Virgo in opposition with a natal or progressed planet in Pisces is an excellent time to get a health checkup.

Costly errors can result from daydreaming during working hours. Check and recheck all instructions, orders, output, and requisitions to avoid confusion.

Be aware and alert to possible deceptive tactics with or through a coworker. You might be tempted to be evasive in filling out certain necessary questionnaires in regards health or work, which is inadvisable. Be careful and avoid possible accidents when handling gas, paint, oil, or chemical products.

For other Virgo aspects, please see the preceding signs.

Chapter Seven

LIBRA

Libra is cardinal and air, noted for peace and harmony. Companionship and sociability in daily activities are very important to these natives, who are active, creative, and ambitious, and have a strong interest in the arts and sciences. Their nature is friendly, obliging, refined, poised, charming, gracious, and diplomatic. However, if heavily suppressed by others, they can become the extreme opposite, and also take by force what they feel is rightfully theirs.

A Libra Planet Conjunction a Planet, Midheaven or Ascendant in Libra

Should this conjunction receive favorable aspects from other planets, the nature is warm and friendly with refinement of manner. The native is altruistically inclined. These people try to see both sides of an issue before judging others or in seeking a decision.

If unfavorably aspected, the native could be vain, self-centered, indecisive, and hot tempered. Trouble is possible in marriage or through business relationships.

In forecasting, the lunation or transiting planet in Libra in conjunction with a natal or progressed planet emphasizes litigation and marriage or business partnerships.

Whether this conjunction produces good results or problematic conditions depends upon other aspects in force at the same time.

A Libra Planet Sextile a Planet, Midheaven or Ascendant in Taurus

Both signs are intellectual, but development in the handling of material matters is needed. Impracticality may be the case, with an easy come-easy go attitude. However, this can be another aspect of protection from material want.

Interest in the arts, literature, and science is possible. This is an excellent placement for a public relations person, diplomat, receptionist, customer service representative, and others who must deal closely with the general public. The nature is kind, tactful, thoughtful, and friendly, and these people value respect, refinement, esteem, and the meeting of influential people.

Gain is possible through marriage or business partners and litigation. Social functions, travel, and influential people can be beneficial to these natives.

In forecasting, social activities, travel, higher education, and religion can prove beneficial at this time. Litigation involving another individual is beneficial in your behalf. News of marriage from someone living in a distant city is possible.

This is a most favored time for meeting influential people. Seek counseling services if necessary. It's also an excellent period to correct past misunderstandings. On the whole, this is a most fortunate time for financial gain and assistance.

A Libra Planet Square a Planet, Midheaven or Ascendant in Capricorn

This is an ambitious combination that is desirous of seeking wealth, prestige, and influence at any cost. The nature may be cold, calculating, reserved, detached, and cynical. Here again, we have fear of rejection to the point where grievances are enlarged out of proportion. There is emotional depression, moodiness, and an outward disposition that generates a certain degree of hardness.

A painful experience resulting through a broken love affair instills mistrust. The native becomes fearful that the marriage partner will also be unfaithful, which can cause some natives to delay marriage. In some cases, marriage is delayed due to responsibility of a parent. This is also an aspect of a May-December relationship, where there is diversity of age.

In forecasting, social functions are hindered or plans go awry. People in general tend to be overly sensitive, easily depressed, and desirous of being left alone.

This is a period during which nothing seems to turn out right. Precious feelings get hurt and result in misunderstandings. Your date cancels, the food in the restaurant is terrible, or you're seated next to a boring person at dinner.

Estrangements through marital or business partnerships and other close personal relationships are possible. You may experience additional responsibility for or have concerns about a parent.

A Libra Planet Trine a Planet, Midheaven or Ascendant in Aquarius

This aspect endows a magnetic, fascinating, charming, and witty personality with loads of sex appeal. Both signs are airy, giving a quick, intellectual, intuitive mentality and an interest in the fine arts or music. The emotions tend to focus on groups rather than one individual. These natives may have frequent and exciting romances, falling in and out of love and enjoying the adventure. This is a popular combination for romantic attraction. Always ready to be of assistance to friends, these natives could be attracted to unconventional associations.

In forecasting, the lunation or transiting planet in Libra in trine aspect with a natal or progressed planet in Aquarius brings exciting and unexpected events. Unexpected gifts are received and invitations to social functions are probable.

New friends can be made and new people met with this stimulating aspect. They will be interesting, magnetic, and somewhat unconventional in behavior. Entering into a partnership with a friend could be considered. On the whole, this is an aspect of unexpected circumstances surrounding conditions in which other persons are involved.

A Libra Planet Quincunx a Planet, Midheaven or Ascendant in Pisces

Secret love affairs and intrigues could be entered into as a means of escaping from reality. Deception from the opposite sex, the mate, or business partner is possible, and secret sorrows through a love affair or marriage could take their toll on the health. In some cases the native might have to care for an ill partner or play the self-sacrificing role with an alcoholic spouse. The nature is impractical and overly concerned with personal pleasures.

In forecasting, this is a good time to encourage your marriage or business partner to seek a medical checkup. A secretive, emotional infatuation may end in disillusionment. Avoid impressionability and permitting others to influence you unfavorably. Before entering into any partnership, take the time to check their reputation. Disreputable characters could enter your life.

For other Libra aspects, please see the preceding signs.

Chapter Eight

SCORPIO

Scorpio is fixed and watery. The emotions are intense and deep. The native strives to keep them under control at all times. A shrewd person with an excellent probing mind. Perfect for vocations requiring penetrative research. May be a perfectionist and sometimes demanding it of others. Strives for power and control over one's immediate environment.

A Scorpio Planet Conjunction a Planet, Midheaven or Ascendant in Scorpio

This intensifies the sexual and emotional feelings, which can be kept under control with favorable aspects from other planets. There is increased willpower, ambition, and the utilization of psychic forces.

Unfavorably aspected, this conjunction can give an obsession for power and the desire to control situations or people. There is an inability to adapt to drastic changes of one's circumstances in life. Violent disputes, quarrels, and a dictatorial attitude toward others is possible. The nature is stubborn, possessive, jealous, and suspicious.

In forecasting, the lunation or transiting planet in Scorpio conjunction a natal or progressed planet increases the fanatical desire for personal achievements. Whether this native goes about it constructively depends upon the aspects this conjunction receives from other planets. In the positive sense, one can make unusual contacts that can promote personal interests. Change is the rule with a Scorpio or Pluto aspect. However, readjustments are readily and easily made. This is an excellent time to make physical changes through diet, exercise, or elimination of bad habits. Money can be gained through the resources of others.

In the negative sense, try to avoid domineering individuals within the environment. You could get involved in an unfortunate or awkward situation. Malicious jealousy, violent disputes and quarrels are possible. A radical change of circumstances could be very upsetting to your plans. A bill you have forgotten to pay could come due, just when you are short of funds.

A Scorpio Planet Sextile a Planet, Midheaven or Ascendant in Capricorn

The frank, sarcastic mannerism of Scorpio is tempered by Capricorn's reserve and self-control. There is excellent organizational ability, willpower, and a mind that can persevere with depth of thought and discipline. The nature is shrewd, tactful, practical, decisive, and concentrative with a sense of duty and love of tradition. This is an excellent placement for interest in scientific fields, medicine, physics, mathematics, and subjects that require deep research. Some of these natives are diplomats, politicians, or government agents.

In forecasting, the lunation or transiting planet in Scorpio sextile a natal or progressed planet in Capricorn brings favorable changes through one's profession as a direct result of past efforts.

Fate (governed by Scorpio) takes a hand in bringing about change of old (Capricorn), existing conditions or through longstanding associations. This native may close the door to one facet of life, while opening the door to another at the same time. Capricorn represents caution, so these changes will be entered into under careful scrutiny and due consideration.

This aspect can aid the native with super strength, endurance, and self-discipline in overcoming the most difficult task or hardship confronting him or her at this time.

Money (Scorpio) through the resources of others (i.e., insurance, health benefits, or an inheritance) that is long overdue (Capricorn) may be forthcoming.

A Scorpio Planet Square a Planet, Midheaven or Ascendant in Aquarius

Scorpio is deeply intense and emotional with a preference for solitude and relationships on a one-on-one basis. Aquarius is mental, with no emotional element. Natives with this combination may become detached in their relationships.

One sign enjoys being with large groups of people; the other doesn't. A square aspect between these two extreme signs can indicate psychological problems. This pulling of the emotional feelings in different directions can make the native overly sensitive. Sometimes the native is uncomfortable in the presence of others, introversion is common, and there is an inability to communicate freely. The native might feel that he or she is different from other people or that something is wrong with him or her. As a rule, the natives outgrow these problems with maturity.

There could be a mental (Aquarius) hang-up about sex, or the very opposite: going to the extreme. The loss of a close friendship through death, relocation, or misunderstanding is possible. There can be unexpected trouble through taxes, alimony, insurance, joint finances, or property of the deceased.

In forecasting, this aspect can bring about a fatalistic (Scorpio) ending, separation, or death of an association, profession, or existing conditions. This is an aspect of upheaval and sudden, drastic changes with far-reaching effects.

Prepare for unpredictable monetary upsets, such as a possible increase in taxes or bills you have forgotten to pay.

Anti-social behavior is possible, along with a desire for isolation or wanting to be left alone. The unexpected loss of a friend or relative is possible.

A Scorpio Planet Trine a Planet, Midheaven or Ascendant in Pisces

This indicates an interest in maritime occupations and sports connected with water. Both signs being of the watery element denotes that shyness, reserve, and love of seclusion is predominant in the nature. The intuition is uncanny and there may be psychic or clairvoyant tendencies. These people have a strong interest in the occult, the mystical sciences, and reincarnation, as well as good mathematical aptitude. The nature is sensitive, impressionable, and easily influenced through their surrounding conditions.

In forecasting, monetary gains through hidden resources are possible, and past errors through a state of confusion can be beneficial to you. For example, a bank statement could reveal an error in your behalf due to wrong calculations in your checkbook or you receive an unusual gift that is handmade or artistically created. It's also possible that an opportunity could open up in which you are able to earn additional money, but for one reason or another you must keep the matter a secret.

For other Capricorn aspects, please see the preceding signs.

Chapter Nine

SAGITTARIUS

Sagittarius is mutable and fiery. The nature is charitable, sincere, fair-minded, and loyal, with religious and moral aspirations. Interested in faraway places, higher education, and travel, honesty and frankness are also characteristic of this sign. However, the native must learn to curb the natural impulse toward being too outspoken. Unlike the Scorpio, the Sagittarius does not intentionally like to hurt anyone's feelings.

A Sagittarius Planet Conjunction a Planet, Midheaven or Ascendant in Sagittarius

This aspect places great emphasis on personal freedom and these natives will rebel at the first sign of restriction. With favorable aspects to this conjunction, the nature is generous, warm, sociable, and sympathetically concerned with the welfare of others. Legal affairs, higher education, and travel will prove beneficial.

If unfavorably aspected, there is dissipation of energy and the scattering of forces, as well as extravagance, misjudgment, and overly expansive ideas. Guard against promising more than you are able to fulfill.

In forecasting, the lunation or transiting planet in conjunction with a natal or progressed planet in Sagittarius means a lucky period lies ahead if other good aspects are in force at the same time.

You could travel or make travel plans for the future. Favorable contacts with in-laws, individuals in distant cities, or foreigners are possible. One may decide to further his or her education. Legal cases can be won. On the whole, Sagittarius can bring success in future enterprises, gain through publications, expansion of present programs, or new opportunities.

Should the conjunction receive difficult aspects, there could be trouble with in-laws, people of different backgrounds, or through a lawsuit. Travel plans may have to be canceled or altered. Business may suffer through misjudgment. Do not take on additional projects until you have completed present ones. Too many irons in the fire can needlessly burn up your energy. Avoid extravagances, overindulgence, and promising more than what you can deliver.

A Planet in Sagittarius Sextile a Planet, Midheaven or Ascendant in Aquarius

Originality is combined with leadership ability. A sextile aspect between the unique Aquarius sign and the Sagittarius power of good reasoning can produce a mind that thinks along lines that are completely different and interesting. These unique ideas can be put to profitable application and bring unexpected gains or good fortune. The nature is intuitive with good insight and prophetic visions. This aspect indicates the makings of a good astrologer because of sound judgment and foresight. There is refinement and sociability on the humanitarian level.

In forecasting, the lunation or transiting planet in Sagittarius sextile a natal or progressed planet in Aquarius means unexpected and unique circumstances bring favorable results with travel, legal matters, and foreign affairs. Publications and religion or higher education bring unexpected surprises.

Sudden windfalls and sudden honors or awards are possible. Expect the unexpected that brings a sudden change of plans. Be ready to use an alternate course if necessary. This trend brings exciting and unlooked-for opportunities. Travel is possible at the last minute. New and unusual friends are made. Legal matters take an unexpected and favorable turn in your behalf. A wider scope of expansion is possible. On the whole, everything takes an upward trend.

A Sagittarius Planet Square a Planet, Midheaven or Ascendant in Pisces

The good judgment and common sense of Sagittarius is distorted by the Pisces emotionalism. This square aspect can produce mental unbalance, extreme nervousness, and emotional disturbances. There is gullibility, unwise choice of friends, and unwise trust in the promises of others, along with a danger of deception, fraud and deceit.

Also possible are secret intrigues with in-laws, foreigners, or those of a different social level than one's own. Be careful of confusion and secrets that can be your undoing in connection with publications, higher education, or lawsuits.

Chaotic or confused conditions can arise while traveling. Use extreme care with food and water when visiting different states or countries. The water or food could be tainted, causing an illness that could require hospitalization.

The nature is sympathetic, sensitive, and optimistic. These natives should learn to finish projects because their attention span is short. Avoid excessive daydreaming and impractical ideas, which can cause you to expand the truth out of proportion.

In forecasting, the lunation or transiting planet in Sagittarius in square aspect with a natal or progressed planet in Pisces means hidden elements, confusion, and chaotic conditions are possible with legal matters, travel, and foreign affairs.

Fraud and deceit are possible in financial matters. Make sure you have all the facts before signing legal documents. Avoid errors of judgment by facing reality and viewing matters as they really are.

For other Sagittarius aspects, please see the preceding signs.

Chapter Ten

CAPRICORN

Capricorn is cardinal and earth. These natives are ambitious, patient, persistent, handle responsibility well, and learn from past experiences. They should learn to bend a little, for they see only one side, their own. Desirous of power, they will use others as a stepping stone if necessary. The nature is careful, practical, conservative, and traditional. They are firm believers in tried and true methods.

A Capricorn Planet Conjunction a Planet, Midheaven or Ascendant in Capricorn

These people have excellent self-control and organizational ability. They are sincere believers in cultural arts, and prefer mingling with prestigious individuals who may be of future benefit to them. Should the conjunction receive unfavorable aspects, there can be the harboring of fears and anxieties, as well as possible dissatisfaction, inhibitions, and a materialistic attitude at the expense of others.

In forecasting, the lunation or transiting planet in Capricorn in conjunction with a natal or progressed planet brings old, stale conditions up for review. Dealings are possible with those in authority, a parent, boss, or government official.

Capricorn and Saturn represent the culmination of old, stagnant conditions. With good aspects to this conjunction, Capricorn can be a good stabilizer. Bringing old conditions to a head that need clearing up, you finally move to new quarters. An old settlement is reached. Or you get a long, overdue promotion.

With unfavorable aspects to this conjunction, old conditions come back to haunt you. Past errors require correcting. Old health problems reappear. Past romances try to rekindle the old flame. Whatever the circumstances, you'll find them tiring and burdensome. A parent could be a source of concern. You could be required to take on additional responsibilities without additional monetary compensation.

A Capricorn Planet Sextile a Planet, Midheaven or Ascendant in Pisces

The disciplined attitude of Capricorn instills good concentration ability to Pisces inspirational ideas. The imagination is focused toward sound and practical ideas. The intuition is sound and dreams become reality. Secrecy could be involved with their career. Some of these natives work behind the scenes for a political or prestigious figure. These natives have a relentless, dogmatic way of ferreting out secret information. The Capricorn reserve and aloofness is softened by the Pisces sympathetic nature.

In forecasting, the lunation or transiting planet in Capricorn in sextile aspect with a natal, progressed, or transiting planet in Pisces brings beneficial help from behind the scenes, and possible assistance or hidden gains through an authoritative figure.

Old, hidden, and confused issues can now be brought out in the open. Ideas, inspiration, and one's imaginative creations can be put to practical use. This is a favorable aspect for those dealing with police activity, hospital work, the mentally handicapped, and government affairs.

A boss may be quietly watching you, admiring the way you handle responsibilities. Self-restraint, caution, and foresight in the methodical manner in which you handle tasks at this time will not go unnoticed.

For other Capricorn aspects, please see the preceding signs.

Chapter Eleven

AQUARIUS

Aquarius is fixed and air. The attitude is colored with original- ity and an advanced mode of thinking. Although the native may be detached and impersonal, there is nevertheless a desire to be with people. The nature is independent with a love of free- dom and enthusiasm for the different, the new, and the uncon- ventional. They love to debate and often take the opposite side, just to stir up an issue. They have good intuition and powers of perception, and are objective in judgment.

An Aquarius Planet Conjunction a Planet, Midheaven or Ascendant in Aquarius

These natives are good speakers and humanitarians, and have a strong interest in scientific fields and astrology. With good as- pects to this conjunction, the native is independent, progressive in thought, modern, and original. Many are thought to be far in advance of the average person. The mind is ingenious with good insight and inventive ability.

Unfavorable aspects to this conjunction can produce a rebel- lious, eccentric, and defiant attitude, as well as an obstinate na- ture and revolutionary tendencies with a passion for innovation. The individual uses unconventional methods and is considered a non-conformist.

In forecasting, emphasis is placed on friends, clubs, and organizations and unexpected and unpredictable circumstances.

Favorable aspects to this conjunction bring new, exciting, and unconventional friends into your circle. There is the possibility of gaining recognition through a club or organization. Exciting events can bring about a change of plans through unusual situations.

On the whole, this is a good period for joining clubs and organizations, attending lectures, exchanging views or ideas, or taking up the study of astrology or the occult sciences.

Unfavorable aspects to this conjunction from other transiting planets can bring loss or separation through a friend. Unexpected accidents or injury are possible. There is a lack of adaptability to upsetting changes that are taking place around you, difficulty with organizations or groups of people, or trouble with gadgets, electricity, television, radio, etc.

For other Aquarius aspects, please see the preceding signs.

Chapter Twelve

PISCES

Pisces is mutable and watery. These natives are very sensitive to their immediate environment and are easily influenced and taken advantage of. They can run the gamut of emotions from self-pity to extremes of temperament. The nature is refined, warm, sympathetic, receptive, sensitive, and compassionate, and there is an inclination to mysticism and artistic pursuits. These natives tend to overstimulate their minds, magnifying problems out of proportion. They should be cautious about abusing alcoholic beverages and drugs.

A Pisces Planet Conjunction a Planet, Midheaven or Ascendant in Pisces

Should this conjunction receive favorable aspects from other planets, the nature will have great sympathy for those afflicted. There is excellent intuition, creative talents, adaptability, idealism and mediumistic ability. These natives work well in vocations connected with institutions, hospitals, and prisons, or with chemical products.

With unfavorable aspects to this conjunction, the native could experience deception, fraud, and deceit or betrayal of confidence. Easily influenced or corrupted by others, there can be a physical weakness or a tendency for drug abuse or alcoholism.

In forecasting, the lunation or transiting planet in conjunction with a natal or progressed planet in Pisces means hidden influences are at work.

Good aspects from other planets to the conjunction can stir an interest in the creative arts, music, dancing, or photography. You might decide to purchase a musical instrument. An unusual gift might be received. Hidden opportunities come to your attention. New, inspirational, and imaginative ideas prove beneficial and productive.

Unfavorable aspects to this conjunction indicate that the native will have to guard against hidden elements of deception. Secret enemies could be working against you. You could hear gossip and rumors about yourself. Someone could become ill and have to enter the hospital. Negative dealings with police are possible. Be careful not to abuse or betray the confidence of another. Do not lay yourself open to the negative influence of others. Do not be a willing servant for the selfish purpose of others.

For other Pisces aspects, please see the preceding signs.